A Fallen Citadel
&
Other Poems

Imali J. Abala

Langaa Research & Publishing CIG
Mankon, Bamenda

Publisher:
Langaa RPCIG
Langaa Research & Publishing Common Initiative Group
P.O. Box 902 Mankon
Bamenda
North West Region
Cameroon
Langaagrp@gmail.com
www.langaa-rpcig.net

Distributed in and outside N. America by African Books Collective
orders@africanbookscollective.com
www.africanbookcollective.com

ISBN: 9956-727-39-3

DISCLAIMER
All views expressed in this publication are those of the author and do
not necessarily reflect the views of Langaa RPCIG.

Table of Contents

Part I: Narrative poems on Kenya's crisis of 2007-2008......... 1
A Fallen Citadel... 3
Birthing of a Nation... 4
Freedom Shall Be Ours... 6
A Disillusioned Youth.. 7
Heaven or Hell?... 8
No End in Sight... 10
Cry Freedom.. 11
Alive Dead Brute... 12
The Unending Cliffhanger.......................................13
The Evil Man... 14
The Victory.. 15
Tribalism.. 16
The Internally Displaced....................................... 17
The Fruits of Uhuru..19
The Corrupt Daughters and Sons of My Mother............. 21
Let My Nation Be My Nation Again!........................... 23

Part II: Other Poems..................................... 25
Eulogy to Maragoli Hills...................................... 27
Lidaala (1).. 28
Lidaala (2).. 29
The Conundrum of My Life.................................... 30
Alone.. 31
Invisible... 32
Defeated... 33
Forever Lost..34
Another Missed Opportunity................................... 35
The 'Joys' of Motherhood...................................... 36
A Woman at the Crossroads................................... 37

An Elderly Widow...38

Daughter of My Mother...39

Dina..40

Fred, the Fallen Star...41

The Orphan Boy..43

The Death of My Son...45

The Boy Who Lived Alone.......................................47

The Maidservant...48

Dead at One...50

Doom's Day..51

Words Hurt..52

A Dying Man's Wish..53

Am I Somebody...54

Hana..56

The Drunkard..59

Have You Ever . . . ?...60

The Bonfire of vanity...62

A Voice at Dawn...63

Part I:
Narrative Poems on Kenya's Crisis
Of 2007-2008

A Fallen Citadel

In the wake of a failed democracy,
A nation stands on a brink of destruction
It, an alien citadel to its citizenry,
Debauched by its elite populace,
Who pillage and plunder its wealth
While its aggrieved poor,
Subjected to police extrajudicial executions,
Seethe in anger as they ruefully mourn
Their fallen citadel of the Lake Basin.

Birthing of a Nation

They marched in droves
Flocked to voting precincts,
Men and women, young and old,
Like gallant soldiers of freedom,
Youthful in their gaiety
Keeping hope abreast.

Yet, their votes fell to the way side,
Slipping into the cracks of corruption,
Erupting a dormant inferno of hatred
from years of suppression
Pitting one ethnicity against another
Pitting neighbour against neighbour
Pitting husband against wife
Rivers of blood of the innocent shed pointlessly,
A sacrifice too painful to fathom.
Kenya, once an island of stability,
Transformed into a land of carnage!

They,
the disenfranchised conscience of a torn nation,
Heckled: No Justice No Peace! No Justice No Peace!
For they understood only to well—
Without democracy, there can be no peace!
Without justice, there can be no peace!
Without freedom of expression, there can be no peace!
Without freedom of mobility, there can be no peace!

Yet, their voices, loud like trumpets,
Fell on deaf ears of politicians,
Their revolutionary march for freedom

Halted in the muck of marauding forces of brute men
Drenched, like hens in a thunderous storm,
Gushed by powerful cannons of water
Strong enough to down the disenfranchised youth
Their budding voices, yearning for freedom, forever silenced.

Yet, out of the ashes of demolition
A new Kenya shall be born
Emerging from the branded fever of violence—
Averting batches of infamy,
of death, of war, of annihilation
A new conscience of solidarity
Shall tether broken hearts
Marking equity the mantra of a new Kenya!

Freedom Shall Be Ours

Freedom shall be ours!
Freedom shall be ours!
Bellowed the youth of a torn nation
Defenseless mercenaries of peace
Who bear the brunt of unemployment
Who bear the brunt of poverty
Who bear the brunt of hopelessness.
Step by step, they marched,
Like dutiful soldiers at a lieutenant's bark,
Thronging the ghostly streets of Nairobi—
Empty, Dead, Broken—
Lured by sweet melodies of hope.
And like accursed simpletons,
They walked into a den of armed brutes!
Alas, the emerging conscience of a torn nation,
Tear gassed by demagogues of power,
Fell one-by-one.
Their broken limbs knew no pain!
Justice shall be ours! Justice shall be ours,
Heckled the youth of a torn nation!

Dimwitted and uniformed,
Demagogues of brute force,
Like actors in a theatre of the absurd,
Plugged their ears, muffling the cries of the fallen,
Closed their eyes to decapitated bodies of the fallen.
Alas, the conscience of a torn nation dead,
Yet, tomorrow,
When they ascend the freedom stairs,
The revolutionary mercenaries of justice,
Shall sing: Freedom is ours!

A Disillusioned Youth

He sits on hard hot asphalt,
lines of dry red crawl on his face,
with a bow and arrow in hand!
His downcast eyes ogle a brown puddle
Broken pieces of plastic scattered around it—
a broken road!
A cool wind gently brushes his brow,
a faint mustache of perspiration appear on his upper lip,
but his mind, wrung like a wet towel,
zooms onto a nation's distant past,
of an ancient history,
where maps of national territories diverged.

His mind, like a field of ruins,
lacks perceptive depth
clouded by a searing storm of anger!
Alas, a memory, knotted like rope,
raped off a constellation of activity,
is permanently paralyzed!
A government's imprisonment of words begin—
Plunging humankind into an abyss of despair
Into a land of darkness,
where old news is but a reminder of a past worth forgetting!
Where new news comes not at all.
Rumors, disguised as news, hardly a luxury.
Ethnic boundaries diverge permanently!

Heaven or Hell?

If there is heaven,
the opiate drug of the masses,
then tell those mothers,
rammed in Jamhuri Park,
jammed in police stations,
like a herd of cattle in a pen,
cold
lonely
hungry
hapless
disoriented
victims of man's inhumanity against man
alone in a world without God
alone in a world without mercy
alone in a world without love!

If there were a heaven,
then hell is here:
chaotic
maddening
saddening
smoking
sizzling
hot
Oblivious men, women, & children watch
as weariness like molten lead
settles in their veins and limbs
their brains, dysfunctional, go numb
a dead day!

If hell were there,
then here now it is,
epitomized by an inferno "furnace"
of houses transformed into crematories
of smells of burning flesh
Alas, there can never be a greater hell than now!

If death were not senseless,
then here now it is.
If life were not meaningless,
then here now it is,
where the innocent pay the ultimate price,
condemned for the sins of their forefathers;
while peacemakers sidelined, watch silently
Alas, there is no heaven, but hell is here now!

No End in Sight

Weeks have come and passed
Months, too, have come and passed,
Years, too, have come and passed,
but the nation's hapless populace disillusioned
still sit in limbo—
forced to drink the bitter dregs of ethnicity,
of a deep rifted socio-political fabric
on a land where the sun is ripe as new bloodshed
where dawn comes, but no day
where a faint beam of hope, at a snail's pace,
lurks on the peripheral in a murk of confusion—
Annan's crib "bugged," a shadowy cloud cast—
but the luckless poor,
trapped like convicts in bands of iron
see not a bright tomorrow!
What a sad epoch in Kenya's humble history!

Cry Freedom Cry

Cry freedom cry—
Sons and daughters of my motherland
Cry freedom cry
For without your tears
We are doomed permanently!

Cry freedom cry—
Sons and daughters of my motherland
Cry freedom cry
For without your heckling
Our voices will forever be silenced!

Cry freedom cry—
Sons and daughters of my motherland
For their voices reverberate
Far and beyond the Lake Basin

Cry freedom cry—
Till your hearts ache of injustice
Cry freedom cry
Till the world awakens
to your struggle
Cry freedom cry!

Alive Dead Brute
(A Policeman's Thoughts)

Shoot the senile brute
You know you want to,
Deep down to your marrow.
Vengeance is sweet, you know!
Come-on, shoot the senile brute.
Even the azure sky knows there is no Peace
The sun, red hot, penetrating, scotching
Pierce your dry ashen skin, no Peace.
Your mouth frothing,
Eyes, blazing with maddening rage,
Blood-thirsting and a vengeful stare
Pierce the senile brute's eyes cowed in cowardice.
Surely, you know you want to annihilate him!
Your finger tightens around the trigger.
The veins in your neck throb.
Your forehead perspires.
Suddenly, a light goes far deeper into your brown eyes
Your finger slips, loosening its grip off the trigger.
He has no conscience—
Alive dead brute.
Save the bullet. Save your soul.

The Unending Cliffhanger

We hang in limbo
On a cliffhanger of anxiety
Our breath suspended
Our guts rumbling like a thunderous storm
Our fate cupped in palms of politicians
Held hostage by a political impasse—
The yoke of our suppression—
Our humanity tethering on a brink
Of slipping into cracks of violence
So,
We gasp
We huff
We puff
We hope
We wish
That if words could move mountains
That if moonlight could dissolve into a *new* dawn
Then, Kenya, our fallen citadel,
Would not totter on the verge of destruction
That if our leaders had a conscience,
Then diplomacy, in the face of disdain,
Would untangle the nation's quagmire
It, an incandescent light,
Reeling us from the cliffhanger of anxiety
From the banality of evil!

The Evil Man

He traded his soul for a bag of fake gold
Glittering in effervescent light
Blind eyes saw not its fakeness
Unclean racing hearts yielded to its allurement
Pontius Pilate hung Humanity on the cross
Dead as though at the alter of pontification
Her drips of red wet mother earth
Dry like the Sahara Desert
God has withheld Her tears
Scraggy men wobble like scarecrow amid a drift
Haggard women sloth around like slobs
With eyes open, empty, vacant, and distant
Scrawny muted children look on questioningly:
Why has God withheld Her tears?
No answer. No food. No nourishment. Nothing
Just the scorching eyes of Nature's wrath
Punishing the innocent
While Pontius Pilate placates his hunger
On his fake gold.

The Victory

The bulls fought
Under the hazy cloud
Under the moonless sky
Of sheer blackness
And the grass suffered
Darkness paved way to dawn
The intensifying sun rose and set
And the earth was bloody
In its setting light
No birds sung in its descent

But an old man sat still
Lapsed into an insulted silence
As his mouth corners frowned rigidly
with embarrassment
Lines of weariness around his eyes emerged
Visible signs of discontent appeared
on his furrowed brow to his mouth
He had lost everything
The game was over and the bulls had won
He understood that fact
No rains of disdain
The grass is dead and shall remain.

Tribalism

Those damned politicians don't get it
Tribalism, the curse of our nation, remains

waving its ugly arms at us
like a tall flower in the wind.

It isn't that they don't get it or don't see it,
but we are alone in our separation.

Even if they ignore,
it won't die it won't go away always there.

Tribalism, the evil cancer of our time,
shall remain time immemorial.

The Internally Displaced

They languished in camps like convicted felons
For crimes they didn't commit. Their world,
Collapsed like dominoes at a finger's touch.
The forgotten victims of a country gone astray,
Dehumanized without mercy,
like creatures devoid of emotional feelings.
Their today empty, like their yesterday;
Their tomorrow, nothing to speak about,
Just another harrowing experience of a lifetime.

They languish in camps,
Praying for Divine intervention
While their leaders look on—
Cruising in luxuriant cars
Carousing in expensive liquor
Placating their hunger on *nyama choma*
As though they were the gods
Up at the pinnacle of their game
Nothing touches them
Nothing affects them
Not even the plight of the displaced
Who suffer the indignity of forced prison life.

Depravation is the mother of indignity,
a wittier woman might have declared!
Perhaps, a politician, pointing theatrically
To all men, women, and displaced children
Simply admits he, too, is a prisoner of prejudice,
which obstructs his conscience's admittance:
Cruelty against man is immoral!
So, he turns a deaf ear to their plight

Closing his mind's eye to their suffering
Let Lot's lot rot in prison, he declares!
What a sad year for the internally displaced.

The Fruits of Uhuru[1]

Wananchi[2] rudely awakened
    rushed to the busy streets of Majengo!
        must they too taste the fruits of Uhuru?
            must they too revel in the luxury of freedom?

Wananchi rudely awakened
    filed on the long *mlolongo*[3] -
        hoping to cash in--
            on the long promised Uhuru!

Wananchi rudely awakened
    sweated on *mlolongo*- till dawn
        but yet saw not the fruits of Uhuru!
            Woke-up by dusk
                but yet reaped not the harvest of Uhuru!

Instead!
 Wananchi bombarded
      with eloquent stories of thievery
         from rippers of the fruits of Uhuru
            were dismayed by the indifference
                of those who carouse on the fruits of Uhuru

Wananchi rudely awakened
    wonder whether they too will feast
        on the fruits of Uhuru.
            After filing on the long *mlolongo* for months,
        a glimpse of hope for the future is almost non-existent.

---

[1] Uhuru in this context could mean independence or freedom
[2] Wananchi are citizens
[3] Mlolongo is a queue

But yet,
    drop! drop! drop! drop!
        the *Wananchi's* sweat
            rain on the dusty tracks of the queue --
                as they struggle to have a taste of Uhuru.

Drop! drop! drop! drop!
    The sweat of *wananchi* may nourish the tree
  but they'll never taste its fruits of independence
        so long as --
            so long as they have remained poor.

Soon the drop! drop! drop! drop!
    Of the sweat of the *wananchi* will soon dry!
            And the well that constantly enriched their pores
                will give way as they'll bond
                    to fight for their fruits of Uhuru that now
                        benefit a few "bumble-clutters."

The Corrupt Daughters and Sons of my Mother

The corrupt sons and daughters of my mother
   Gloat in smothering affluence
      Yet, isn't their destiny my destiny?

The corrupt daughters and sons of my mother
   take the little I have
      preaching the holy gospel saying:
         Those who have plenty will be rewarded
         and those who have little,
        will have the little they have taken away from them
         yet, aren't we all one?

The corrupt daughters and sons of my mother
   rejoice at seeing me walk in tattered clothes
     with dirt on my back too thick to overlook
       and my ashy hands itching for a small drop of oil
      yet, aren't we the same blood?

The corrupt daughters and sons of my mother
   spit in my face
     denying my very existence
       as though we didn't come from the same womb!

The corrupt daughters and sons of my mother
   watch my hungry children
     whose faces are covered with flies
       buzzing around their dirty mouth
        licking sap from yesterday's sugar cane
        mucus oozing from their nose
         while their blood relatives look on
       their bellies protruding from their shirt buttons

                    yet, aren't we from the same womb?

The corrupt daughters and sons of my mother
        watch my children struggle to bury my corpse
            in a coffin that only halfway covers my remains
                watching my legs protrude at the lower end—
                    saying "just wrap his body in banana leaves
                        so we can sell the wood for a profit—"
                                They break the bones of my corpse
                                forcing me into a case-like coffin
                                    least they be burdened by the expense
                    forgetting we came from the same womb!

These daughters and sons of my mother
        forget that when they are old
            and their youthfulness has left their body
                they, like me, will face their Maker
                    as we all will.

And you daughters and sons of my mother
        aren't we all mortals?
                Daughters and sons of my mother
                    we all will have to answer to our ancestors--
                after all, we are all sons and daughters of our mother.

Let My Nation Be My Nation Again

Let my nation be my nation again
a country where diverse nations reside
coexisting with ease
a country without the deftness of death
a country where the souls of its inhabitants
are pure, clean, loving
a country where our lost humanity is not trite

Let my nation be my nation again
a land where politicians do not bicker inanely
a land where time is not at a standstill
a land where lights are not out
a land where transportation is not dead
a land where the roads are not broken

Let my nation be my nation again
a nation where the faces of its subjects are at peace
where sadness on their visage
is not imprisoned in their flesh by the wind
where the masses move harmoniously
like water in the streets,
not out of fear of a machete's cut
not out of fear of an arrow etched in the flesh

Let my nation be my nation again
where peaceful hearts reside!

Part II:
Other Poems

Eulogy to Maragoli Hills
(When Nature Is Destroyed)

She sits
quietly,
defiantly,
naked
in a mournful fright.
Geckos bob their heads
on her hard dry bare surface
a monkey hops—
step
 by
step
slide
slip
grip
No tree here!
No safety net here!

Heartbreaking,
dreadful,
blip,
she flops downwards
busting her head;
red splatters
white splatters
baptize the
hard cold stone
No tree here!
No safety net!

Lidaala[4] (1)
(A Giant Rock at the Base of Maragoli Hills)

She stands tall and erect
her sharp grey edged grooves
are nothing, but an eye sore.
Multiple rings of brown
decorate her base;
red sandy pebbles
loosely drift off her
amid a slight waft
arghr
Acacia could've saved her.

Water glides down
her sharp edged ridges,
clear to her base;
tilt tipper
boom
she bolters
awkwardly downwards
in a thunderous storm.
Wham bam,
she hobbles along,
rolling like a rabid dog.
No security net here!

---

[4] **Lidaala** a name of a giant boulder.

Lidaala (2)

Gargantuan,
flat,
slippery,
enticing,
she sits melancholically.
Uncountable rings of brown
violently wrap her belly
like a chain on a prisoner's anklet,
a silent victim of man's greed.

The Conundrum of My Life

I died long before I knew my name
Long before I muttered my first syllable
Long before I lost my first tooth
Long before I was submerged in the Holy books
Long before I shed my first blood
Long before I lost my innocence
So, don't ask me why I am not myself
I was indoctrinated to despise my tongue
I was indoctrinated to hate my ebony skin
I was indoctrinated to be ashamed of my short hair
I was indoctrinated to loathe my unschooled mother
I was indoctrinated to abhor my flesh and blood
Thus, I fell into the chasms of knowledge
And like a bat in a daylight flight
Fell into the *pure* and *unadulterated* Faith of the West
Fell head over heels in love with my modern education
Fell prey to the tight-jean mentality of my youth
Fell into the mini-skirt traps of my adolescent life
Fell into the romantic love traps of the West
Never having learned a thing of substance of my culture
Therefore, don't cry for me
For your tears will be wasted
A dead woman is not worth a tear
A dead existence is nothing to fret over
I died long before I knew my name
Long before I produced an heir
Long before I was put six feet under
For there, in the depth of earth,
I shall forever remain
Unknown
Unacknowledged!

Alone

She sits by the riverside
her tired feet dangling in cool water
weary with sadness, drifting, alone

her mind, like a boat down stream,
overwhelmed with duty and feeling,
drifts away not caring who tries to dock.

Invisible

Silence permeates my life:
Seen, but not seen
Never seeing in my looking
Absent even in my presence
Unheard even in my utterance
Voided even in my accolades
Dead even in my living
My voice, beautiful like a song bird's,
Sings, but is muted in my vocalization
Bitter-sweetness of an invisible life
Me, woman, black!

Defeated

I am paralyzed with defeat,
An omnipresent family philanthropist,
Pulled down by the yoke of dependency
No way to lift those drowning in poverty.

Forever Lost

I wanted to go back
I wanted to belong
Not buoyed in the world—
A desolate planet—
Aimlessly roving, not docking
A slave to the universe
Not docking—
Hypocrisy is my garb.

I wanted to go back
I wanted to belong
But my blackness hampered me
Me, a slave of the universe,
No freedom—surrendered
Never docking—
Hypocrisy is my garb
And shall remain—
Undocked, disarmed, lost!

Another Missed Opportunity

She raved like a rabid dog
In dregs of her past
As anger, tantamount to hate,
Weighted her heart
Her red hot eyes bulged
Her nose dripped like a spring
Her ears, hot like a flaming rod, burnt
From the fervent equatorial heat
Her tender skin baked in a taint of brown
No kind eyes anywhere
No solace of any sort for her lot
Fallen from the pedestal of innocence
Adam's cassava too good to resist
Beguiled, yet again,
But he, with his tail coiled
Between the valley of his legs,
Smiled gleefully
Another grand accomplishment
And vanished into oblivion
As for her, she remained pensive—
Another missed opportunity.

The 'Joys' of Motherhood

He crept out of her timely
He, an epitome of her joy,
Small, delicate, lovely
An anchorage of her life, finally!

But that joy, only short lived,
Gave birth to batches of infamy
Of hours of being nudged like an ass
Of tender breasts sucked like rubber
Bitten without mercy
Of constant cries of hunger
Of constant cries of illness—
Forced her to muse the unthinkable
Of bottoms that need wiping
Of the nose that needs wiping—
Made her gag in disgust
Of sleepless nights now her daily curse—
Made her restless
And from the depth of her heart
She felt no joy
No third light could make her see *it*
Why had God punished her?
Why had she to suffer for Eve's sin?
Perhaps, mother should have warned her:
"There is no joy in motherhood, my child,
Just another dreaded lifetime sentence!"

A Woman at the Crossroads

She spread-wide her dry calloused hands
Her empty palms, wide open like a shovel,
Reveal dry ashen fingers, fat like an udder,
Her long-browned nails curve at the tips like a bow,
    a hallmark of defeat
Besides her, two pale-faced forms awkwardly stand,
their four imposing drills penetrate her soul
She has nothing to offer them, zilch, nada—
Dry grey lines crawl from their nose to mouth
Leaving a snail-like trail
Then, a left frail bony wire stretches out,
Touching her fat ashen udders
Two unmistakable crystal beads pop-out of her eyes,
Which remain distant and vacant,
Instantly, in her mind's eye, she *knows*:
He has forgotten her and her sorry lot!
Nothing else happens,
Just a pregnant silence!

An Elderly Widow

Tradition had robbed her life
Tradition had robbed her education
Tradition had robbed her income
Tradition had robbed her voice
Tradition had robbed her vitality
Now, she sits on an old broken wicker chair,
Art of his labor, like an ebony stub,
Under a dark cloud of her living
Gripped with a longing gaze
Her heart thumps like an old clock's ticking
While her eyes keep vigil of the gate
Forever hoping against hope that he'd return
But he lies six feet under, undisturbed
And she is alone, empty, defeated!

Daughter of My Mother

The lost daughter of my mother
quietly sits in remonstration,
her hollow eyes,
as round as Sodom Apples,
shyly hide behind rims of her
 eyelids;
her dark brown pupils goggle
            into distant horizons
'free at last, free at last,'
            she gasps,
'mind, body, and soul!'
Yet,
invisible shackles of femininity
pull her down, down, down
until she vanishes into oblivion—
A squashed bug.

Dina

I did not weep
when Dina died—
for I had no tears
left in my eyes;
I had shed them
days before she passed on
I had not bid her farewell—
our sweet mother, beacon of hope!
I did not know at the time of parting
that it was a parting in itself
Mama had told me she was dying of old age,
but that was just a sham
her children had abandoned her,
denying her medical intervention—
for she deserved no treatment,
old age was an illness undeserving cure.
So I cried and cried and cried
till the wells of my tears dried
not that she was dying,
but because her ungrateful children,
without concern for the ailing mother,
had lost their moral compass,
their conscience, dead
like the stiff of their mother,
forgetting that Dina,
in the prime of her youth,
had nursed them to life
while she, in old age, had been denied life.

Fred, the Fallen Star

I was tongue-tied
mind boggled
when I saw him—
a young stunted in growth
frail thin legged dry-skinned
brown marasmus Fred—
and didn't say anything.

Bare footed, he must have trekked
the treacherous three mile journey,
left home at the twilight of dawn,
when dark clouds shrouded the mountains,
his brown innocent eyes sparkling in light
hoping against hope.
It wasn't knowledge that ignited his odyssey,
but the turbulent roiling of his stomach.

So, he tumbled into me like a fallen star
in the crumbling of light
his hope and fear infusing my world.
Yes, he tripped and stumbled, unaware,
youthful, in the obscurity of my life
his eyes gaping into mine
like ghosts from my past
and like an automaton, my hand
reached for a ladle and,
digging into a torrid pot,
spooned him a morsel.
And now I am left to sing his song,
a song of the forgotten fallen star,
hoping against hope that he'll survive.

The truth is
Fred's scrawny image torments me.
It won't stop playing on my mind
like a movie from the theatre of the absurd.
And under all his drifting world of pain,
the frail thin legged marasmus Fred,
yearning to be fed
remain bitter in the black tide of his life.
How much longer can he sustain life on nothing?

The Orphan Boy

He sits on my lap
quietly like a helpless lamb
trying to understand
life's cruel realities
of a mother's absence.

As I gaze into his eyes,
with a sense of keenness,
like a doctor examining
her patient on an operating table,
I try to understand
what he must be thinking:
The loss of his mother,
of the motherly love he'll never know.

As I gaze into his eyes again,
overcome with his empty stares,
A hollow feeling of deep sadness engulfs me,
making my stomach cramp like a woman in labor:
It is as if he were inquisitively asking me "why?"

Tiny drops of uncontrollable tears
pave their way down my cheeks.
As I stare in his eyes with emptiness
I want to say to him:
"Son, I, too, do not understand
Why nature's lessons are too harsh,
merciless to the innocent
who might profit from a mother's embrace."

Moved by protective love,
my hands begin to find their way
through his coarse unkempt hair,
wondering why the child should have been
orphaned at such a tender age.
As warm tears continue to form in my eyes,
I am reminded of the cruel realities of life
He must feel.
But I, an aunt,
who bears a close resemblance
to his mother, wonder
if my mere presence isn't
an agonizing reminder of a mother he'll never know.
I wonder if I, a sister of his mother,
could be a stranger to him
just like any woman on the street.
So, I weep for him
while his empty eyes
Look into my teary eyes
as though asking me, "Why do you weep?"
So, I stroke his head
wondering if he understands it is he for whom I weep.

I pull his malnourished body to my breast
and feel the tension in his body dissipate
as he calmly buries his head in my bosom,
Reminding himself of the warmth he misses,
The tenderness he yearns for,
And within minutes of peace,
The gentle hands of sleep claim him
As he drifts away into a deep slumber
while I sadly look for a scarf
to wipe tears off my face.

The Death of My Son

I killed my son yesterday,
locking him in a cultural linguistic prison;
how devastating his death had been!
He stood no chance at life
for I had decided his fate
long before he knew his name,
long before he could utter a word,
casting him in a dungeon of no return.
Forever dead! Forever dead! Forever dead!
His tongue, tied to his adopter's foreign tongue,
Sweet, sour, bitter!
Yes, I had uprooted the roots of his lineage,
killing his ancestors unknowingly
for with his tongue tied,
his link to his past dies with me.
For he knows only his imitated Queen's mores,
forced to live in a disarming tranquility of ignorance
oblivious to his culture,
he, an uprooted simpleton in the name of Progress.

I should have known of his untimely death
for the white owl had proclaimed it
by its sinister hooting cry,
carrying with it a foreboding fervor of doom.
So I picked-up a burning splinter,
threw at it forcefully, with full hope
that stopping its sinister cry
would, just slightly, alter my son's fate,
but the owl had already taken flight in fright,
vanishing into the depth of sky
covered with grey clouds

pregnant with droplets of water,
but that was just a façade
for owl returned momentarily with a fiery fury
when my eyes were closed in prayer
descending towards earth like a storm
howling like the mightiest beast known to man
mocking me with its hooting yet again.
So I killed my son,
locking him in a cultural linguistic prison
where he was alienated from himself
where he was alienated from his family
where he was alienated from his kinsmen,
but the white owl still sung mockingly,
staying true to its nature
Yet, my son was dead and shall remain;
the death of humanity, *our* death.

The Boy Who Lived Alone

Boomeranged
catapulted
like an arrow in a bow
buoyed like a yoyo
he stands alone;
held by an ancient silence
words timelessly detained in his dry throat
his sad angry eyes
crawl behind his curly eyelashes
unseeing, unfeeling, uncaring
no third eye could redeem him now
he, the lost son of woman,
and the boy who lived alone wonders:
'Is life worthy living?'

The Maidservant

I quit my job today—
It was the best decision I ever made,
The first time ever I used my mind.
What an exhilarating feeling!
Never again shall I be a dishrag
To that fat-pot-bellied nitwit disease infected
Beer stinking, tobacco chimney boss of mine.

I quit my job today—
It was the best decision I ever made!
Never again shall I listen to my mistress' nagging—
Scolded without cause
Humiliated without reason
Starved without mercy
What a debilitating experience.

I quit my job today—
It was the best thing I ever did!
Never again shall I suffer my mistress' indignity
For she laughed at me
Pointed a finger at me
As though I were scum
A cow-dung imbecile without brains
"Don't ever lament to me you filthy wench
You stinking goat from Kakamega!"
So, I hang my head in shame.

I quit my job today—
It was the most liberating decision I ever made.
Never again shall I be scorned by my mistress!
As I near the end rope of my life,

I, daughter of woman, have suffered the injustice of life.
For poverty had robbed me of an education.
For poverty had robbed me of the joy of youth,
Sodomized at the hand of my pot-bellied
Beer stinking good for nothing boss of mine
For poverty had robbed me of happiness
For poverty had robbed me the joy of motherhood
For poverty had robbed me of life
Infected with HIV at a tender age of 15,
Now death smiles at me with open arms,
As wide as the eyes can see, to receive me.
I have no choice in the matter
Just as much as I had none in life.

So I quit my job today—
It was the most liberating thing I ever did.
And as I walked out of my mistress' house,
I raised my eyes into the skies
The clouds looked like cotton balls gliding with ease
And the browned zinc-tainted roof tops
Of an unwelcoming city looked like a wasteland
Of a dead past like the dreams of my formative years
So I closed my eyes, sealing my fate forever
Ending a life lived in disharmony.

Dead at One

She was too young to understand life's truths
too young to know its hardships
too young to grasp inhumanity
too young to realize her human rights.
As hunger gnawed her,
poverty goaded her parents' defeat.
When tragedy struck her family unexpectedly,
She, a mere infant, aged one—
at a healer's divination—
fell from the pedestal of innocence
at her father's hand under the death trap of AIDs.
Her purity, a miracle cure for an incurable malady.
Now, she, a wasted face of AIDs,
Sits in her parents' shanty shambles
'Dreaming' of a dawn to ripen her hopes
Amid the muck of utter hopelessness
Alone, dead to an unforgiving world
Never having lived long enough to realize life's beauty!

Doom's Day

It was a dawn like no other, calm, still, sinister
The moon, hidden behind dark clouds, appeared not
Suddenly, violent winds begun to howl
Like howling wolves in the night
Dry leaves rustled under its violent bluster
Nervous dogs barked in terror
And, at the calm of the tumultuous roar,
A sinister silence gripped earth:
The frogs were soundless
The crickets were soundless
The birds were soundless
A forceful menacing calm remained
Roosters did not crow to summon dawn
A bloody red sun weeping rose
Relentless, burning, angry
Countless carcasses floated downstream
Like barges of forbidden cargo
People's shamed red-hot eyes dropped to the ground
Fathers' wells of bloody tears dried at last
Mothers, writhing with pain, cried
but no tears appeared
Man's inhumanity exposed
The yoke of modern day atrocities
gripped earth mercilessly
Doom's day at last, the end!

Words Hurt

He sharpened his pen,
Poisoning its tip
And like a spitting cobra,
He flicked his tongue
Spitting venom of malice
Against my veritable ponderous cogitation
My freedom of thought decimated in a flash
Buried in a dust cobwebbed coffin—
Of dead rhymes never to reemerge.

How easily it had been,
For him to unmake me
Exposing my dry bones
His obliterating exegesis
Merely vomit of an adulterated mind
Easy to destroy,
But unwilling to nurture
Easy to dismiss,
But unwilling to embrace
A bitter prisoner of his mind
Yet, my dreams swift and magnificent
Stand still at the center of my heart.

A Dying Man's Last Wish

He'd come down with malaria—
Gagging and bile puking—
His frail body, laced with goose bumps,
Shivered like a leaf under the sunny sky
Its warmth, no match to his teeth's clamor
Tucked underneath a brown blanket,
His tan skin was invisible to the eye
Save for his eyes fixed on me like two drills
He tried to speak, but his teeth chattered
Then forcefully, he mumbled:
"If only you could give me some intestines,
It'll make me feel better
And I'd forever be indebted to you!
You don't have to slaughter chicken,
Just its intestines and a Fanta will suffice."
And then, he was gone!

Am I Somebody?

I once had a dream—
to be somebody.
Father told me:
If you want to be somebody,
get the white man's education!
And like a dutiful daughter, I listened
emulating an old song mama once sang to me:
I want to learn
I want to learn
I want to learn
I want to learn
Till I go to Europe
So I did!
What a misguided quest!
Days came and passed
Weeks came and dissolved into months
Months dissolved into years
My resolve resolved.
Yet, am I somebody?

Mama in her old age said gleefully:
That is my educated daughter.
But, Permanent Head Damage,
the hallmark of my success,
has left me at the alter of Confusion
shunned for my accomplishment.
No children!
No husband!
Was a dream fulfilled
worth more than a dream differed?

Now,
I sit in my bungalow alone
sipping piping coffee.
My body—
wrapped in a fleece's throw—
warms-up.
No human touch.
A muted telly light—
my only linkage to humanity—
flashes on endlessly.
And I, in my silence, wonder:
Am I somebody?

Hana

Her beauty is like a blossomed Pear tree!
Her full bloomed body,
Her long dark hair,
Her bright charming brown eyes,
Her smooth soft ebony skin,
And her long neck
Depict an angelic portrait of Hana.
Her elegant walk
Invites spectators to a gaze;
her full blossoming figure,
too enticing to miss,
draw them to a halt
as though she were a ripe peach ready for plucking.
Men's hungry eyes undress her without mercy,
while we women are drawn to anger,
loathing her every whim.
As her soft angelic lips move,
slowly, carefully, and mechanically,
uttering her first word of *mulembe*[5],
we are all taken aback.
Her sweet tender voice
too soothing to ignore.
So we hang tightly onto each syllable of her word,
entranced by the tenderness of her voice.
Alas, we realize our mouths are gaping
our eyes drooping
and our minds wondering where
Such tenderness of heart emerged.
Her simple smile

---

[5] Mulembe means peace in Logooli language

sends our hearts racing
and the palpitation of our hearts drumming.
Suddenly we realize in our gaze,
We had forgotten a simple courtesy—
to return her greetings—*mulembe*.
And so we wonder out loud:
"Why are we puzzled by her?"
"Why are we fascinated by her?"
"Why do we marvel at her?"
Eyeball to eyeball,
we search in her innocent,
yet captivating eyes
to see if we can understand
that which has drawn us to her.
Only to realize that it is
her charm, elegance, and naiveté
we find attractive.
But soon,
we gaze in her eyes again
searching for that brilliant light,
but, sadly, we begin to see
the radiance in them fading,
reminding us that
the sun had began to withdraw
Her claws lights
slinking them
way back beyond Mt. Elgon
leaving a red tear
etched across the blue sky
and only emptiness in Hana's eyes.
Eyeball to eyeball,
we look into those big brown eyes
again as we wonder

at the red-hot rays we now see,
not the kind of red that makes one
grow vivid inside and out—passion
but, void, a lack of brilliance and sparkle
we once sought.
Yet, despite the fading luster in her eyes,
we are drawn to her,
as her simple politeness and elegance
that had once drawn us to her
prevent us from abandoning her.
And so we hover around her
hoping to ignite in her eyes
the fire we had once found irresistible.
And soon, the moon
serenely envelops her
in her coat of dim lights
her face charred permanently,
a sad reminder to us of the warmth
Mother Earth gives her troubled
children, soothing their wounds forever!

The Drunkard

A bald gray-haired drunkard stands alone
Buoyed by the tide of time
Forever moving, never docking
His sunken cheeks, deep like a canyon,
Expose his bony cheekbones
Hollow-eyed like a starved knave—
A dead-walking grave—
He has weathered many a storm
His lips, cracked like the crevices of his heels,
Gape wide, revealing two brown-crooked fangs
He, a thorny-bowlegged slob,
    A *changaa* guzzling drum-bellied bum,
    A reefer puffing snob,
Looks on
His frail bony hands poke his belly
That protrudes like an over-inflated balloon—
No match to a worm-bellied marasmus child—
His timid eyes recoil behind his blinking wires
Once knotted with sleep-matter
Inebriated, he collapses . . . a nincompoop
And time marches on at a steady pace,
Never stopping . . .

Have You Ever . . .?

Have you ever been in a position-
    in which you knew not
        where your daily bread comes from?

Have you ever been in a position -
      where you were constantly taunted by persons in power
        but yet knew not where to go or to whom to turn?
        (See your husband)[6]

Have you ever been coerced - -
  or thrust into a situation in which
  your bare existence depended upon your physical attributes?

Have you ever been in a position ---
    in which opening your legs
        is supposed to boost your ego
            up the ladder of social mobility?
            (Women are obedient, loyal,
                patient, and submissive to authority)

Then you know ----
    a woman's dismal plight.
      From sexual harassment----
        (no! Means yes!, they like it)
          low wages----
            (women's salaries are supplementary)
              to crude remarks ----
                (hire docile -- subservient women without self-
confidence, outspoken and self confident women

---

[6] all sections in italics refer to subliminal messages

are troublemakers)

And you still think----
      my place, our place
           or my position, our position as women is easy?

The Bonfire of Vanity

Blazing flames
Of the burning disc of the sun
Hot
Steaming irresistible
Maddening
Passion
Love

Cool
Smooth
Sweet
Tasty
Passion
Maddening lust
Good

Hot
Sizzling heat
Sweat
Salty
Rolling
Wet
Damp
Ecstasy

A Voice at Dawn

at dawn
I sing a song of my liberty
as the lurking star
points a finger in the East
eminence of my freedom

at dawn
I hum a tune of my deliverance
as the fingers of the morning Sun point eastward
a sign of my hope for a bright future

at dawn
I hear the sweet melodies of birds
as they chirp morning tunes
showering my day with gladness
a sign of my new-found voice

at dawn
I spring out of bed,
wakened by the brightness of the shooting star,
guided by the fingers of the morning Sun,
and given a voice by the chirping birds

at dawn
I now know
I have a voice
and will not be silenced.